CT Simulator
Lab Book

First Edition

Ken Meacham, PhD (RT)(R)(CT)(MR), CRA, CPSA, CIIP
President, The Institute for Advanced Clinical Imaging

THE INSTITUTE FOR
ADVANCED CLINICAL IMAGING

The CT Simulator Software

The CT Simulator software was designed to provide clinical hands-on training to students within the classroom. While we have worked to make this product as life-like as possible, some functions are too complex to simulate. However, we do believe we have developed an outstanding learning tool. For more information and to demo this product visit: **www.iacionline.com/simulators.da.**

+

The CT Simulator Lab Book

This lab book was designed as a companion to the CT simulator software developed by The Institute for advanced clinical imaging (IACI) . These products were developed in direct response to feedback provided by the MRI and CT students of IACI. I am extremely grateful to all of the students whose feedback has been invaluable to the improvement of our programs. For more information about the programs at IACI visit: **www.iacionline.com.**

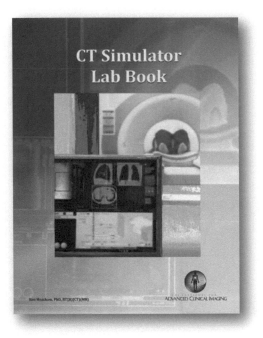

The Institute for Advanced Clinical Imaging
1114 Highway 96, Suite C1-322, Kathleen, GA 31047
www.iacionline.com
Email: info@iacionline.net

Objective:
In this lab you will create an account and navigate the features and options associated with the CT Simulator.

Step - By - Step
1. On the computer desktop, double click on the **CT simulator icon** to open the login form.

2. On the login form, click on the button labeled **"Need to Register**?" This will open the student registration page.

3. In the fields provided, enter the requested information then click the **Register button**.

NOTE: This will create a login account that will also be used by the instructor to track student activity.

4. Click the **OK button** on the message prompt that states "New account was registered." This will take you to the login page again with your new username and password already loaded.

5. Click the **Login button** to log into the primary CT simulator console.

6. Take a moment to review the buttons and settings on the primary CT scanner console.

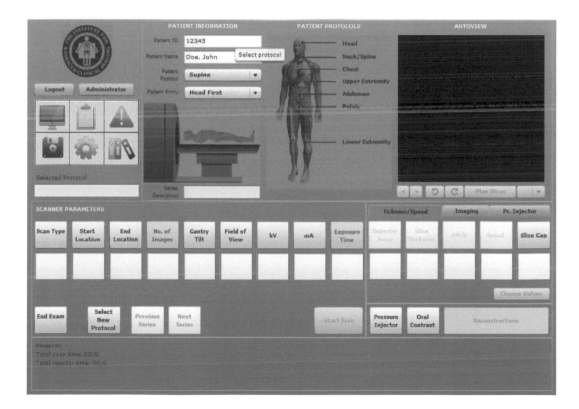

7. Click on the **IACI logo**. This will take you to the website of the institute for advanced clinical imaging. http:/www.iacionline.com. The users can contact IACI utilizing the Contact Us page.

8. These buttons are inactive and simulate other functions found on an CT scanner. However, they are not necessary part of learning to scan.

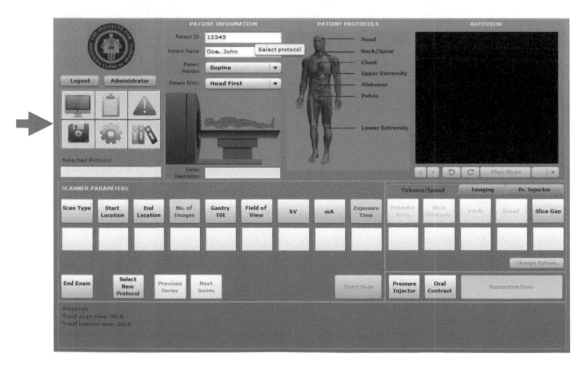

9. This area is used to store the demographic information of the patient being scanned. Enter a patient ID of 1234 and the patient name of Doe, John.

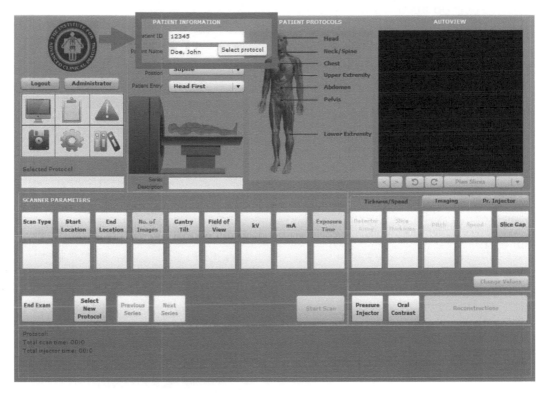

10. This area of the console includes patient positioning.

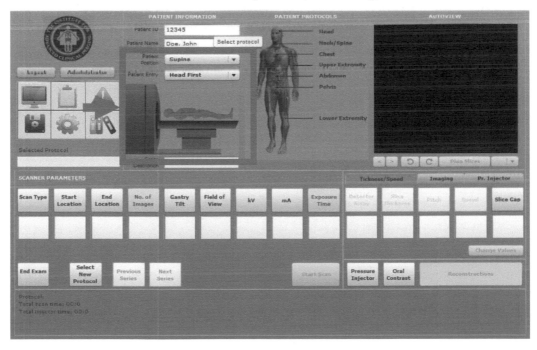

11. In the patient position area click on the **Patient Position button** and select Prone. Then click on the **Patient Entry button** and click feet first. Notice that the graph displays the selected patient orientation.

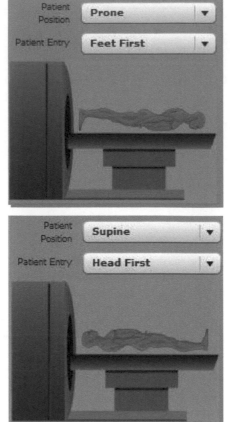

12. Change the patient's position back to Supine, Head First.

13. On the patient protocol panel, click the Head button to display the protocols used to scan an CT of the head.

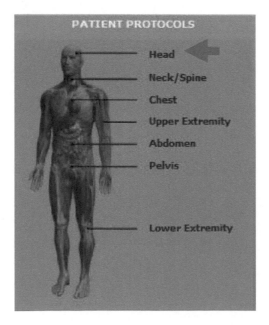

14. Click and highlight the **first head protocol** in the protocol selection panel. Once highlighted, click the **Select button** on the bottom right of the protocol window. This will load the parameters necessary to scan a CT of the head.

Anatomical Reference	Protocol Name	Series
Head	Head test	2
Head	Lab 2 Head	4
Head	Lab 3 Head	2
Head	Lab 4 Head	2
Head	Lab 5 Sinuses	2

Select Protocol ✕

Protocols

Cancel Select

15. Notice the series description loaded in the series description area of the CT simulator console.

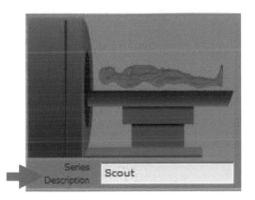

16. Also notice the parameters required to perform a scout series are loaded.

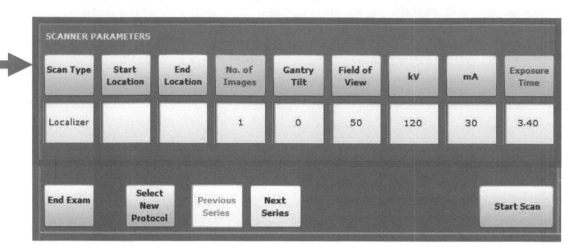

17. Hover your mouse over the **kV parameter button**. Notice the parameter description appears.

18. Click on the button labeled **kV** and select 120 from the list. Click the Save button to save the value.

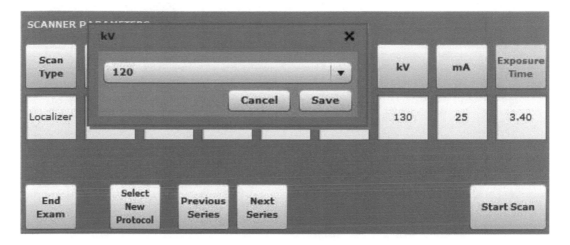

19. Click on the button labeled **mA** and change the mA parameter to 30. Click

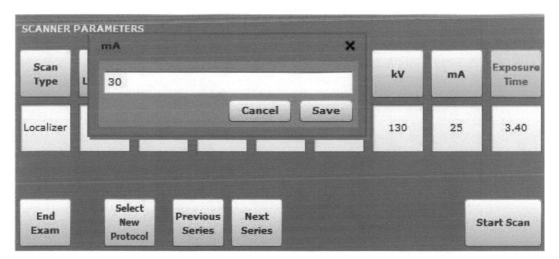

the save button to save the value.

20. Notice the parameters included on the **Thickness/Speed tab**.

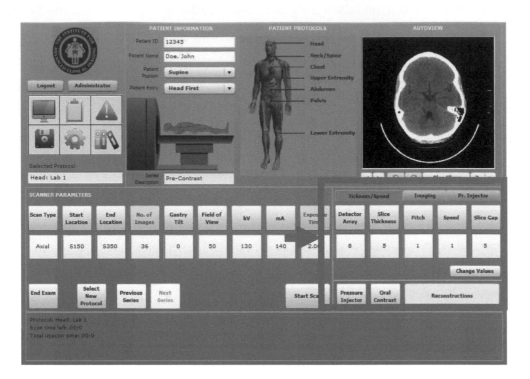

21. Click on the **Change Values button** to view and change the thickness and speed values. Each individual parameter button can be clicked to change the individual values as well.

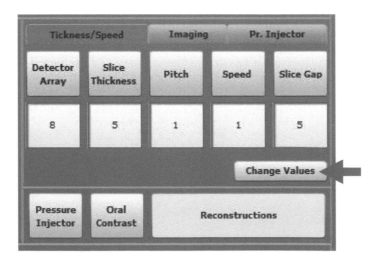

22. Notice the parameters in this window. Select **16** detector rows and click the **Save button**.

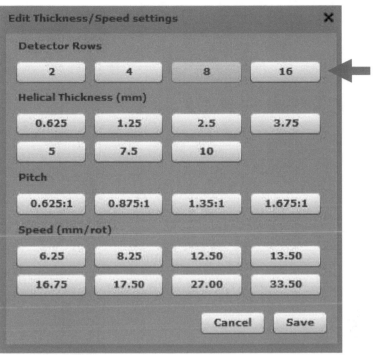

23. Click on the **Imaging Tab**. Notice the parameters that can be changed on this tab. Click the **Reconstruction Algorithm button** and select Soft Tissue.

24. Click the **Start Scan button**. Notice the scan progress. After the scan is complete, the scout image will appear in the autoview window.

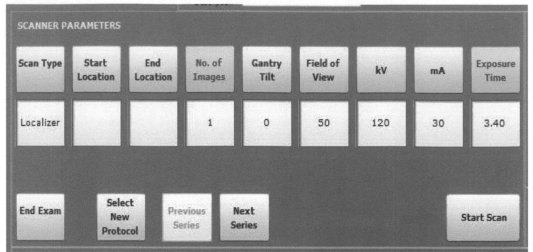

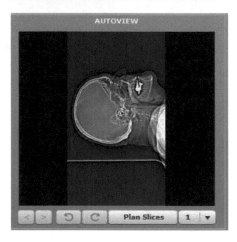

25. Once the scout image has been displayed, click the **Next Series button**. Notice the parameters have changed to an axial sequence.

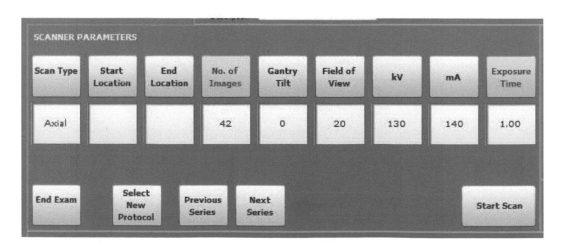

26. Utilizing the **left mouse button**, click on the image and drag the mouse. Notice that the **Window/Level** changes the appearance of the image. Adjust the window/level until the image appears best.

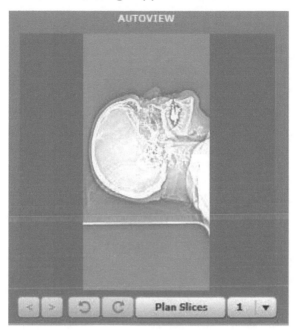

27. Click on the **Plan Slices button** to activate the slice planning function for the axial sequence.

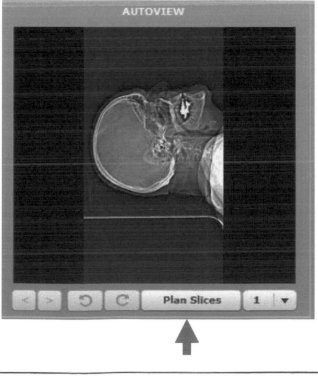

28. Utilizing the **left mouse button**, click and drag the mouse from the base of the skull to the vertex. Use the circular arrow buttons to angle the slices parallel to the supraorbital meatal line. Click the **End Planning button**.

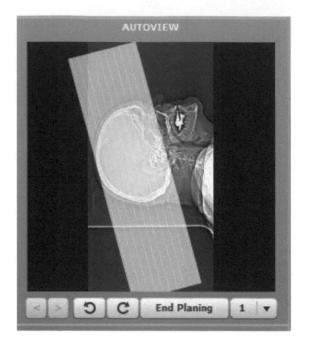

29. Notice the values for Start Location, End location, and Gantry Tilt have been assigned.

Scan Type	Start Location	End Location	No. of Images	Gantry Tilt	Field of View	kV	mA	Exposure Time
Axial	S141	S305	42	15	20	130	140	1.50

SCANNER PARA ERS

End Exam | Select New Protocol | Previous Series | Next Series | Start Scan

30. Click on the **Pr. Injector Tab**. In the PH1 row, Click on the **Side field** and activate injector side A and click the save button. Click in the **Flow field**, enter 2 and click the save button. Click on the **Volume field** enter 100 and click the save button.

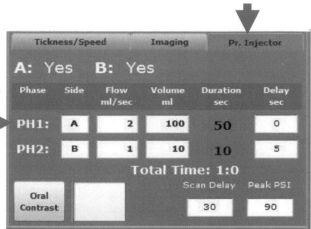

31. In the PH2 row, Click on the **Side field** and activate injector side B and click the save button. Click in the **Flow field**, enter 1 and click the save button. Click on the Volume field enter 10 and click the save button. Click on the **Delay field** and enter 5. Click on the Scan Delay field enter 30 and click the Save button. While the PSI field can be changed, it defaults to 90 psi.

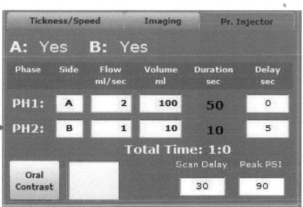

32. Click the **Start Scan Button**.

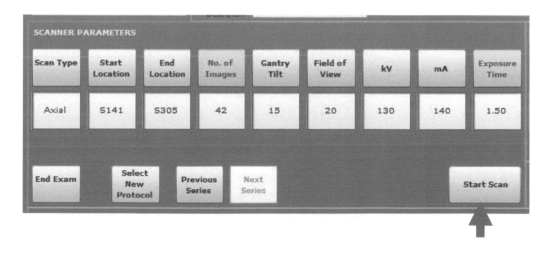

33. Once the scan completes, images will display in the **Autoview window**. Once the image reconstruction completes, click the **Next >** and **Prior <** buttons to move through the scanned images. Click these buttons to review the images.

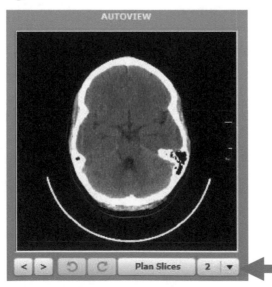

34. The student can navigate back to the scout series by selecting the series number dropdown box on the autoview window. Click the series button and select series 1 to view the scout image. Click this button again to select series 2 and review the axial images.

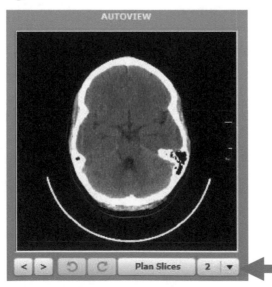

35. Multiplanar reconstructed images can be made by clicking on the **Reconstruction button** at the lower right corner of the simulator screen.

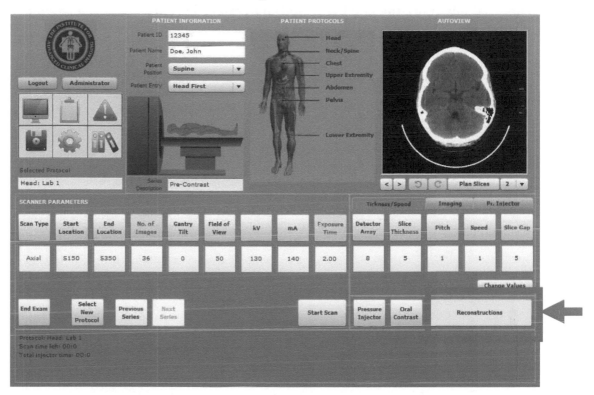

36. To generate multiplanar reconstructed images, the student must select the plane and reconstruction algorithm and enter the field of view, slice thickness, and slice spacing. Once these parameters are entered, the student can draw the appropriate slices by clicking the plan slices button and drawing the slices. After this is done, reconstructed slices can be created by clicking the apply button.

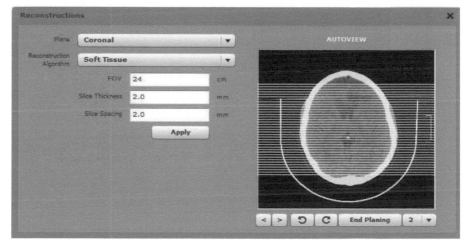

* It should be noted that this is a simulated function and not all sequences have simulated reconstructed images in every plane.

36. The **Logout** button logs the student out of the simulator program. The **End Exam** button clears all of the fields and prepares the CT simulator program for a new patient. Click the **End Exam** button to clear the fields. Click the **Logout button** to log out of the software.

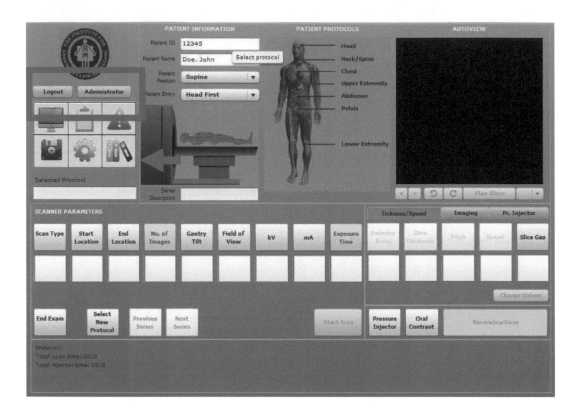

37. Please complete the questions on the following pages.

Simulator Questions

1. Describe how scan protocols (labs) are selected utilizing the simulator.

_____

_____

_____

_____

_____

2. Describe how scanning parameters (kVp, mA) are changed utilizing the simulator?

_____

_____

_____

_____

3. Describe how image slices are planned using the simulator?

_____

_____

_____

_____

_____

_____

_____

4. Describe how the pressure injector is setup and utilized?

_____

_____

_____

_____

_____

_____

5. Which area of the simulator displays the images after they have been scanned?

_____

_____

_____

_____

_____

6. How can the student window and level the image?

_____

_____

_____

_____

_____

7. Describe how reconstructed images are created?

_____

_____

_____

_____

_____

_____

_____

8. How can a student find the IACI website?

_____

_____

_____

_____

_____

CT Head Without & With Contrast

Objective:

In this lab you will screen the patient, scan an CT of the head without & with contrast, and evaluate the images.

Patient Information

Patient: Johnson, Anna
Age: 25
History: 25 year old female with a history of right sided headaches times 2 weeks.
Referring Physician: Samuel Smith, MD

I. PATIENT SCREENING:

A. Evaluate the patient requisition.

B. Evaluate and sign the patient's screening form.

C. Answer the patient screening questions.

II. PERFORM EXAM:

A. If there are no contraindications, enter the patient's name and demographic information into the simulator and continue the exam performance steps. If there are contraindications, please halt the study.

B. Scan the protocol listed on page 4. Upon the completion of each sequence evaluate the images for artifacts and pathology.

C. Answer the procedure questions.

General Medical Center
Patient Requisition

Patient ID		Accession Number	
41256832		CT1505101739	

Last Name	First Name	Referring Physician
Johnson	Anna	Smith, Samuel, MD

Age	Gender	Phone	Exam
25	F	(478)555-0202	CT Brain Without & With Contrast

History

25 y/o female with right sided headaches times 2 weeks.

BUN	Creatinine	GFR	
17.0	0.9	76.0	

Notes

GENERAL MEDICAL CENTER
CT Screening Form

Patient Name: _Anna Johnson_   **Referring Physician:** _Dr. Sam Smith_

Sex: ☐ Male ☑ Female   **Height:** _51"_   **Weight:** _125 lbs_   **Age:** _25_

Are you pregnant? ☐ Yes ☑ No ☐ N/A   **Last menstrual period:** _____

Please explain the reason for which you are having a CT exam:
Severe headaches on the right side for two weeks

List other medical problems: _None_

List any drug and/or food allergies: _None_

Are you taking Gluaphage? ☐ Yes ☑ No   **BUN** _17.0_   **Creatinine:** _0.9_   **eGFR:** _76.0_

Have you ever had a previous allergic reaction to x-ray contrast (dye)? ☐ Yes ☑ No

Have you been pre-medicated for this exam? ☐ Yes ☑ No

Do you have or have you ever had any of the following?

☐ Yes ☑ No Asthma
☐ Yes ☑ No Allergic Respiratory Disease
☐ Yes ☑ No Diabetes
☐ Yes ☑ No Kidney Disease
☐ Yes ☑ No Cancer
☐ Yes ☑ No Multiple Myeloma
☐ Yes ☑ No Prostate Problems
☐ Yes ☑ No Are you breast feeding at this time?
☐ Yes ☑ No Dizziness
☐ Yes ☑ No Heart Disease
☐ Yes ☑ No Stroke
☐ Yes ☑ No Liver Disease
☐ Yes ☑ No Seizure Disorder
☐ Yes ☑ No Bladder Disease
☑ Yes ☐ No Headaches

List Previous Surgeries:
None

List Medications Currently Taking:
None

I attest that the above information is correct to the best of my knowledge.

X _Anna Johnson_

Patient/Parent/Legal Guardian   **CT Technologist's Signature**   **Date**

FOR TECHNOLOGIST USE ONLY

Type of contrast: _____   **Contrast Temperature:** _____

Lot Number: _____   **Expiration Date:** _____

Time of Injection: _____   **Amount:** _____

Protocol

Protocol: CT Head Without & With Contrast

Parameters	Scout	Pre Contrast	Post Contrast
Patient Position	Supine	Supine	Supine
Patient Entry	Head First	Head First	Head First
Scan Type	Scout	Axial	Axial
Scan Plane		Transverse	Transverse
IV Contrast	N/A	N/A	100 mL @
IV Contrast Timing	N/A	N/A	1 mL/s
IV Contrast Scan Delay	N/A	N/A	5 minutes
Oral Contrast	N/A	N/A	N/A
Reference Angle		Parallel to Supraorbital Meatal Line	Parallel to Supraorbital Meatal Line
Scan Field of View	Large Body	Large Body	Large Body
Display Field of View	23cm	23cm	23cm
Start Location		Just Below Skull Base	Just Below Skull Base
End Location		Just Above Vertex	Just Above Vertex
Algorithm		Soft Tissue	Soft Tissue
Reconstruction Slice Thickness		5mm	5mm
Slice Spacing		5mm	5mm
KV		120	120
MA		150	150
Detector Rows		16	16

Slice Reference

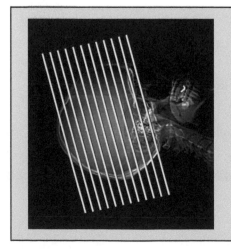

Transverse slices of the brain should be planned with angulation in the slices parallel to supraorbital meatal line. This angulation reduces the radiation dose to the orbits.

Patient Screening Questions:

1. Is the exam ordered consistent with the patient's history and symptoms? If not, describe why they are not consistent.

_____

_____

_____

_____

_____

_____

_____

_____

2. Are there any contraindications that would prevent the patient from having a CT exam? If so, list and describe each.

_____

_____

_____

_____

_____

_____

_____

_____

3. Are there any items found on the patient screening form that could cause potential artifacts? If so, please describe.

_____

_____

_____

_____

_____

_____

_____

_____

Exam Performance Questions

4. What is the patient's orientation?

_____

_____

_____

_____

5. Why is it preferable to set up the slices parallel to the supraorbital meatal line rather than the orbital meatal line?

_____

_____

_____

_____

6. Were there any artifacts on the images? If so, list the artifact name, list the sequence it appears on, describe its appearance, and define how it should be corrected.

_____

_____

_____

_____

_____

_____

_____

_____

7. Was there any pathology found on the images? If so, list the sequence it appears on and describe its appearance.

_____

_____

_____

_____

_____

_____

_____

_____

NOTES

NOTES

CT Head Without Contrast

Objective:

In this lab you will screen the patient, scan an CT of the head without contrast, and evaluate the images.

Patient Information

Patient: Jackson, William
Age: 43
History: 43y/o male s/p MVA 1 week ago. Extreme confusion and left sided headaches since accident
Referring Physician: Lindsey McCown, MD

I. PATIENT SCREENING:

A. Evaluate the patient requisition.

B. Evaluate and sign the patient's screening form.

C. Answer the patient screening questions.

II. PERFORM EXAM:

A. If there are no contraindications, enter the patient's name and demographic information into the simulator and continue the exam performance steps. If there are contraindications, please halt the study.

B. Scan the protocol listed on page 4. Upon the completion of each sequence evaluate the images for artifacts and pathology.

C. Answer the procedure questions.

General Medical Center
Patient Requisition

Patient ID		Accession Number	
41256833		CT1505101740	

Last Name	First Name	Referring Physician
Jackson	William	Lindsey McCown, MD

Age	Gender	Phone	Exam
43	M	(478)555-0303	CT Brain Without Contrast

History

43y/o male s/p MVA 1 week ago. Extreme confusion and left sided headaches since accident.

BUN	Creatinine	GFR	

Notes

GENERAL MEDICAL CENTER
CT Screening Form

Patient Name: _William Jackson_   **Referring Physician:** _Dr. Lindsey McCown_

Sex: ☒ Male ☐ Female   **Height:** _59"_   **Weight:** _175 lbs_   **Age:** _43_

Are you pregnant? ☐ Yes ☐ No ☒ N/A   **Last menstrual period:** _____

Please explain the reason for which you are having a CT exam:
Car accident 1 week ago. Since the accident I have had extreme confusion and severe headaches.
_____

List other medical problems: _None_

List any drug and/or food allergies: _None_

Are you taking Gluaphage? ☐ Yes ☒ No **BUN** _____ **Creatinine:** _____ **eGFR:** _____

Have you ever had a previous allergic reaction to x-ray contrast (dye)? ☐ Yes ☒ No

Have you been pre-medicated for this exam? ☐ Yes ☒ No

Do you have or have you ever had any of the following?   **List Previous Surgeries:**
None

☐ Yes	☒ No	Asthma
☐ Yes	☒ No	Allergic Respiratory Disease
☐ Yes	☒ No	Diabetes
☐ Yes	☒ No	Kidney Disease
☐ Yes	☒ No	Cancer
☐ Yes	☒ No	Multiple Myeloma
☐ Yes	☒ No	Prostate Problems
☐ Yes	☒ No	Are you breast feeding at this time?
☒ Yes	☐ No	Dizziness
☐ Yes	☒ No	Heart Disease
☐ Yes	☒ No	Stroke
☐ Yes	☒ No	Liver Disease
☐ Yes	☒ No	Seizure Disorder
☐ Yes	☒ No	Bladder Disease
☒ Yes	☐ No	Headaches

List Medications Currently Taking:
None

I attest that the above information is correct to the best of my knowledge.

x _William Jackson_   _____   _____
Patient/Parent/Legal Guardian   **CT Technologist's Signature**   **Date**

FOR TECHNOLOGIST USE ONLY

Type of contrast: _____   **Contrast Temperature:** _____

Lot Number: _____   **Expiration Date:** _____

Time of Injection: _____   **Amount:** _____

Protocol

Protocol: CT Head Without Contrast

Parameters	Scout	Pre Contrast
Patient Position	Supine	Supine
Patient Entry	Head First	Head First
Scan Type	Scout	Axial
Scan Plane		Transverse
IV Contrast	N/A	N/A
IV Contrast Timing	N/A	N/A
IV Contrast Scan Delay	N/A	N/A
Oral Contrast	N/A	N/A
Reference Angle		Parallel to Supraorbital Meatal Line
Scan Field of View	Large Body	Large Body
Display Field of View	23cm	23cm
Start Location		Just Below Skull Base
End Location		Just Above Vertex
Algorithm		Soft Tissue
Reconstruction Slice Thickness		5mm
Slice Spacing		5mm
KV		120
MA		150
Detector Rows		16

Slice Reference

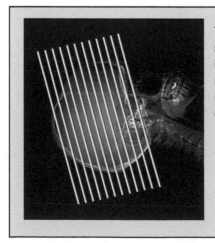

Transverse slices of the brain should be planned with angulation in the slices parallel to supraorbital meatal line. This angulation reduces the radiation dose to the orbits.

Patient Screening Questions:

1. Is the exam ordered consistent with the patient's history and symptoms? If not, describe why they are not consistent.

_____

_____

_____

_____

_____

_____

_____

_____

2. Are there any contraindications that would prevent the patient from having a CT exam? If so, list and describe each.

_____

_____

_____

_____

_____

_____

_____

_____

3. Are there any items found on the patient screening form that could cause potential artifacts? If so, please describe.

_____

_____

_____

_____

_____

_____

_____

_____

Exam Performance Questions

4. Were there any artifacts on the images? If so, list the artifact name, list the sequence it appears on, describe its appearance, and define how it should be corrected.

_____

_____

_____

_____

5. Was there any pathology found on the images? If so, list the sequence it appears on and describe its appearance.

_____

_____

_____

_____

_____

6. When is a non-contrast CT of the brain indicated?

_____

_____

_____

_____

_____

7. Tissue plasminogen activator (t-PA) is a treatment for acute ischemic stroke. When is this treatment contraindicated?

_____

_____

_____

_____

_____

NOTES

NOTES

CT Head With Contrast

Objective:

In this lab you will screen the patient, scan an CT of the head with contrast, and evaluate the images.

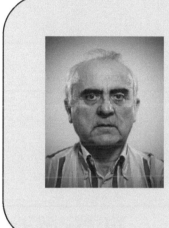

Patient Information

Patient: Schneckenburger, Walter
Age: 71
History: 71 y/o male with altered mental status, blurred vision, and headaches
Referring Physician: Morgan Grindstaff, MD

I. PATIENT SCREENING:

A. Evaluate the patient requisition.

B. Evaluate and sign the patient's screening form.

C. Answer the patient screening questions.

II. PERFORM EXAM:

A. If there are no contraindications, enter the patient's name and demographic information into the simulator and continue the exam performance steps. If there are contraindications, please halt the study.

B. Scan the protocol listed on page 4. Upon the completion of each sequence evaluate the images for artifacts and pathology.

C. Answer the procedure questions.

General Medical Center
Patient Requisition

Patient ID	Accession Number
41256834	CT1505101741

Last Name	First Name	Referring Physician
Schneckenburger	Walter	Morgan Grindstaff, MD

Age	Gender	Phone	Exam
71	M	(478)555-0404	CT Head With Contrast

History

71 y/o male with altered mental status, blurred vision, and headaches.

BUN	Creatinine	GFR	
19.00	1.10	66.00	

Notes

GENERAL MEDICAL CENTER
CT Screening Form

Patient Name: _Walter Schneckenburger_   **Referring Physician:** _Dr. Morgan Grindstaff_

Sex: ☑Male ☐ Female   **Height:** _5'8"_   **Weight:** _150 lbs_   **Age:** _71_

Are you pregnant? ☐Yes ☐No ☑N/A   **Last menstrual period:** _____

Please explain the reason for which you are having a CT exam:
Altered mental status, blurred vision, headaches
_____

List other medical problems: _Lung cancer_

List any drug and/or food allergies: _Penicillin_

Are you taking Gluaphage? ☐Yes ☑No   BUN _19_   Creatinine: _1.1_   eGFR: _66_

Have you ever had a previous allergic reaction to x-ray contrast (dye)? ☐Yes ☑No

Have you been pre-medicated for this exam? ☐Yes ☑No

Do you have or have you ever had any of the following?

☑Yes	☐No	Asthma
☐Yes	☑No	Allergic Respiratory Disease
☐Yes	☑No	Diabetes
☐Yes	☑No	Kidney Disease
☑Yes	☐No	Cancer
☐Yes	☑No	Multiple Myeloma
☐Yes	☑No	Prostate Problems
☐Yes	☑No	Are you breast feeding at this time?
☑Yes	☐No	Dizziness
☐Yes	☑No	Heart Disease
☐Yes	☑No	Stroke
☐Yes	☑No	Liver Disease
☐Yes	☑No	Seizure Disorder
☐Yes	☑No	Bladder Disease
☑Yes	☐No	Headaches

List Previous Surgeries:
Upper left lung removal

List Medications Currently Taking:
None

I attest that the above information is correct to the best of my knowledge.

X _Walter Schneckenburger_   _____   _____

Patient/Parent/Legal Guardian   **CT Technologist's Signature**   **Date**

FOR TECHNOLOGIST USE ONLY

Type of contrast: _____   **Contrast Temperature:** _____

Lot Number: _____   **Expiration Date:** _____

Time of Injection: _____   **Amount:** _____

Protocol

Protocol: CT Head With Contrast

Parameters	Scout	Post Contrast
Patient Position	Supine	Supine
Patient Entry	Head First	Head First
Scan Type	Scout	Axial
Scan Plane		Transverse
IV Contrast	N/A	100 mL @
IV Contrast Timing	N/A	1 mL/s
IV Contrast Scan Delay	N/A	5 minutes
Oral Contrast	N/A	N/A
Reference Angle		Parallel to Supraorbital Meatal Line
Scan Field of View	Large Body	Large Body
Display Field of View	23cm	23cm
Start Location		Just Below Skull Base
End Location		Just Above Vertex
Algorithm		Soft Tissue
Reconstruction Slice Thickness		5mm
Slice Spacing		5mm
KV		120
MA		150
Detector Rows		16

Slice Reference

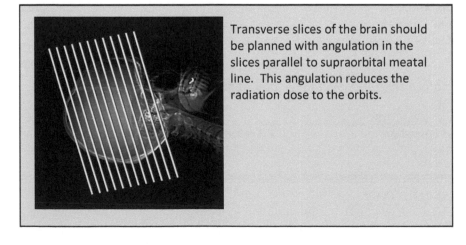

Transverse slices of the brain should be planned with angulation in the slices parallel to supraorbital meatal line. This angulation reduces the radiation dose to the orbits.

Patient Screening Questions:

1. Is the exam ordered consistent with the patient's history and symptoms? If not, describe why they are not consistent.

_____

_____

_____

_____

_____

_____

_____

_____

2. Are there any contraindications that would prevent the patient from having a CT exam? If so, list and describe each.

_____

_____

_____

_____

_____

_____

_____

_____

3. Are there any items found on the patient screening form that could cause potential artifacts? If so, please describe.

_____

_____

_____

_____

_____

_____

_____

_____

Exam Performance Questions

4. Were there any artifacts on the images? If so, list the artifact name, list the sequence it appears on, describe its appearance, and define how it should be corrected.

_____

_____

_____

_____

_____

_____

_____

_____

5. Was there any pathology found on the images? If so, list the sequence it appears on and describe its appearance.

_____

_____

_____

_____

_____

_____

_____

_____

6. List 3 common widow/level settings utilized to visualize cross-sectional slices of the brain. Identify what each setting is used to visualize.

_____

_____

_____

_____

_____

_____

_____

_____

NOTES

NOTES

CT Screening Sinuses

Objective:

In this lab you will screen the patient, scan an CT screening sinuses, and evaluate the images.

Patient Information

Patient: Janelle Simmons
Age: 32
History: 32 y/o female with headaches & congestion for 3 months.
Referring Physician: Sidney Samson, MD

I. PATIENT SCREENING:

A. Evaluate the patient requisition.

B. Evaluate and sign the patient's screening form.

C. Answer the patient screening questions.

II. PERFORM EXAM:

A. If there are no contraindications, enter the patient's name and demographic information into the simulator and continue the exam performance steps. If there are contraindications, please halt the study.

B. Scan the protocol listed on page 4. Upon the completion of each sequence evaluate the images for artifacts and pathology.

C. Answer the procedure questions.

General Medical Center
Patient Requisition

Patient ID	Accession Number
41256832	CT1505101739

Last Name	First Name	Referring Physician
Simmons	Janelle	Minh-Yen Ly, MD

Age	Gender	Phone	Exam
32	F	(478)555-0505	CT Screening Sinuses

History

32 y/o female with headaches & congestion for 3 months.

BUN	Creatinine	GFR	

Notes

GENERAL MEDICAL CENTER
CT Screening Form

Patient Name: _Janelle Simmons_   **Referring Physician:** _Dr. Minh-Yen Ly_

Sex: ☐ Male   ☑ Female   **Height:** _5'7"_   **Weight:** _140 lbs_   **Age:** _32_

Are you pregnant? ☐ Yes   ☑ No   ☐ N/A   **Last menstrual period:** _____

Please explain the reason for which you are having a CT exam:
Headaches & congestion for 3 months

List other medical problems: _None_

List any drug and/or food allergies: _None_

Are you taking Gluaphage? ☐ Yes   ☑ No   **BUN** _____   **Creatinine:** _____   **eGFR:** _____

Have you ever had a previous allergic reaction to x-ray contrast (dye)? ☐ Yes   ☑ No

Have you been pre-medicated for this exam? ☐ Yes   ☑ No

Do you have or have you ever had any of the following?

			List Previous Surgeries:
☐ Yes	☑ No	Asthma	_Tonsillectomy_
☐ Yes	☑ No	Allergic Respiratory Disease	
☐ Yes	☑ No	Diabetes	
☐ Yes	☑ No	Kidney Disease	
☐ Yes	☑ No	Cancer	
☐ Yes	☑ No	Multiple Myeloma	
☐ Yes	☑ No	Prostate Problems	**List Medications Currently Taking:**
☐ Yes	☑ No	Are you breast feeding at this time?	_Medrol dose pack_
☐ Yes	☑ No	Dizziness	
☐ Yes	☑ No	Heart Disease	
☐ Yes	☑ No	Stroke	
☐ Yes	☑ No	Liver Disease	
☐ Yes	☑ No	Seizure Disorder	
☐ Yes	☑ No	Bladder Disease	
☐ Yes	☑ No	Headaches	

I attest that the above information is correct to the best of my knowledge.

X___ _Janelle Simmons_ ___   _____   _____
    Patient/Parent/Legal Guardian   **CT Technologist's Signature**   **Date**

FOR TECHNOLOGIST USE ONLY

Type of contrast: _____   **Contrast Temperature:** _____

Lot Number: _____   **Expiration Date:** _____

Time of Injection: _____   **Amount:** _____

Protocol

Protocol: CT Screening Sinuses

Parameters	Scout	Pre Contrast
Patient Position	Prone	Prone
Patient Entry	Head First	Head First
Scan Type		Axial
Scan Plane		Coronal
IV Contrast	N/A	N/A
IV Contrast Timing	N/A	N/A
IV Contrast Scan Delay	N/A	N/A
Oral Contrast	N/A	N/A
Reference Angle		Perpendicular to the orbital meatal line
Scan Field of Vew		
Display Field of View	23cm	16cm
Start Location		Mid sella turcica
End Location		Through the frontal sinus
Algorithm		Soft Tissue
Reconstruction Slice Thickness		2.5 mm
Slice Spacing		2.5 mm
KV		120
MA		150
Detector Rows		16

Slice Reference

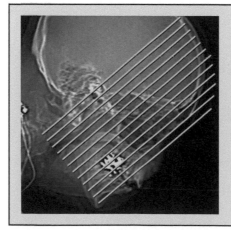

Coronal slices of the sinuses should be angled perpendicular to the orbital meatal line. The slices should cover the anatomy from the center of the sella turcica through the frontal sinuses.

Patient Screening Questions:

1. Is the exam ordered consistent with the patient's history and symptoms? If not, describe why they are not consistent.

_____

_____

_____

_____

_____

_____

_____

_____

2. Are there any contraindications that would prevent the patient from having a CT exam? If so, list and describe each.

_____

_____

_____

_____

_____

_____

_____

_____

3. Are there any items found on the patient screening form that could cause potential artifacts? If so, please describe.

_____

_____

_____

_____

_____

_____

_____

_____

Exam Performance Questions

4. Were there any artifacts on the images? If so, list the artifact name, list the sequence it appears on, describe its appearance, and define how it should be corrected.

_____

_____

_____

_____

_____

_____

_____

_____

5. Was there any pathology found on the images? If so, list the sequence it appears on and describe its appearance.

_____

_____

_____

_____

_____

_____

_____

_____

6. Describe the benefits of performing an screening sinus study rather than a complete sinus study?

_____

_____

_____

_____

_____

_____

_____

_____

NOTES

NOTES

CT Neck With Contrast

Objective:

In this lab you will screen the patient, scan an CT of the neck with contrast, and evaluate the images.

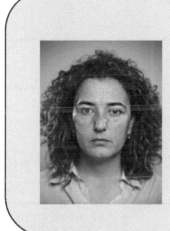

Patient Information

Patient: Elizabeth Anderson
Age: 45
History: 45 y/o female with sore throat x 6 months
Referring Physician: Julian Campbell, MD

I. PATIENT SCREENING:

A. Evaluate the patient requisition.

B. Evaluate and sign the patient's screening form.

C. Answer the patient screening questions.

II. PERFORM EXAM:

A. If there are no contraindications, enter the patient's name and demographic information into the simulator and continue the exam performance steps. If there are contraindications, please halt the study.

B. Scan the protocol listed on page 4. Upon the completion of each sequence evaluate the images for artifacts and pathology.

C. Answer the procedure questions.

General Medical Center
Patient Requisition

Patient ID		Accession Number
41256832		CT1505101739

Last Name	First Name	Referring Physician
Anderson	Elizabeth	Julian Campbell, MD

Age	Gender	Phone	Exam
45	F	(478)555-0606	CT Neck With Contrast

History

45 y/o female with sore throat x 6 months.

BUN	Creatinine	GFR	
18.0	1.0	60.0	

Notes

GENERAL MEDICAL CENTER
CT Screening Form

Patient Name: _Elizabeth Anderson_   **Referring Physician:** _Dr. Julian Campbell_

Sex: ☐ Male ☑ Female   **Height:** _5'5"_   **Weight:** _111 lbs_   **Age:** _45_

Are you pregnant? ☐ Yes ☑ No ☐ N/A   **Last menstrual period:** _____

Please explain the reason for which you are having a CT exam:
Sore throat for 6 months

List other medical problems: _Sinusitis_

List any drug and/or food allergies: _Eggs_

Are you taking Gluaphage? ☐ Yes ☑ No   **BUN** _18.0_   **Creatinine:** _1.0_   **eGFR:** _60.0_

Have you ever had a previous allergic reaction to x-ray contrast (dye)? ☐ Yes ☑ No

Have you been pre-medicated for this exam? ☐ Yes ☑ No

Do you have or have you ever had any of the following?   **List Previous Surgeries:**
Sinus surgery

☐ Yes ☑ No Asthma
☐ Yes ☑ No Allergic Respiratory Disease
☐ Yes ☑ No Diabetes
☐ Yes ☑ No Kidney Disease
☐ Yes ☑ No Cancer
☐ Yes ☑ No Multiple Myeloma
☐ Yes ☑ No Prostate Problems   **List Medications Currently Taking:**
☐ Yes ☑ No Are you breast feeding at this time?   _Lexapro_
☐ Yes ☑ No Dizziness
☐ Yes ☑ No Heart Disease
☐ Yes ☑ No Stroke
☐ Yes ☑ No Liver Disease
☐ Yes ☑ No Seizure Disorder
☐ Yes ☑ No Bladder Disease
☑ Yes ☐ No Headaches

I attest that the above information is correct to the best of my knowledge.

X _Elizabeth Anderson_ _____   _____   _____
  Patient/Parent/Legal Guardian   **CT Technologist's Signature**   **Date**

FOR TECHNOLOGIST USE ONLY

Type of contrast: _____   **Contrast Temperature:** _____

Lot Number: _____   **Expiration Date:** _____

Time of Injection: _____   **Amount:** _____

Protocol

Protocol: CT Neck With Contrast

Parameters	Scout	Post Contrast
Patient Position	Supine	Supine
Patient Entry	Head First	Head First
Scan Type		Helical
Scan Plane		Transverse
IV Contrast	N/A	125 mL @
IV Contrast Timing	N/A	1.5 mL/s
IV Contrast Scan Delay	N/A	2 minutes
Oral Contrast	N/A	N/A
Reference Angle		Angle Gantry Parallel to the hard palate
Scan Field of View		Large Body
Display Field of View	23cm	18cm
Start Location		Mid Orbit
End Location		Clavicle Heads
Algorithm		Soft Tissue
Speed (mm/rot)		12.5
Reconstruction Slice Thickness		2.5mm
Slice Spacing		1.25mm
Pitch		0.625
KV		120
MA		150
Detector Rows		16

Slice Reference

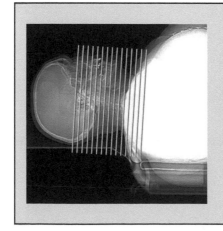

Axial slices of the neck should be oriented parallel to the hard palate. The slices should cover the anatomy from mid orbit to the clavicular heads.

Patient Screening Questions:

1. Is the exam ordered consistent with the patient's history and symptoms? If not, describe why they are not consistent.

_____

_____

_____

_____

_____

_____

_____

2. Are there any contraindications that would prevent the patient from having an CT exam? If so, list and describe each.

_____

_____

_____

_____

_____

_____

_____

3. Are there any items found on the patient screening form that could cause potential artifacts? If so, please describe.

_____

_____

_____

_____

_____

_____

_____

Exam Performance Questions

4. Were there any artifacts on the images? If so, list the artifact name, list the sequence it appears on, describe its appearance, and define how it should be corrected.

_____

_____

_____

_____

_____

_____

_____

_____

5. Was there any pathology found on the images? If so, list the sequence it appears on and describe its appearance.

_____

_____

_____

_____

_____

_____

_____

_____

6. Define "split bolus" injection technique and describe its use in CT exams of the neck.

_____

_____

_____

_____

_____

_____

_____

_____

NOTES

NOTES

CT Cervical Spine Post Myelogram

Objective:

In this lab you will screen the patient, scan a CT of the cervical spine post myelogram, and evaluate the images.

Patient Information

Patient: Margaret Walker

Age: 52

History: 52 yo female s/p cervical myelogram

Referring Physician: Bettina Hawkins, MD

I. PATIENT SCREENING:

A. Evaluate the patient requisition.

B. Evaluate and sign the patient's screening form.

C. Answer the patient screening questions.

II. PERFORM EXAM:

A. If there are no contraindications, enter the patient's name and demographic information into the simulator and continue the exam performance steps. If there are contraindications, please halt the study.

B. Scan the protocol listed on page 4. Upon the completion of each sequence evaluate the images for artifacts and pathology.

C. Answer the procedure questions.

General Medical Center
Patient Requisition

Patient ID	Accession Number
78958	CT789582349

Last Name	First Name	Referring Physician
Margaret	Walker	Bettina Hawkins, MD

Age	Gender	Phone	Exam
52	F	(478)555-0707	CT Cervical Spine

History

52 y/o female s/p cervical myelogram

BUN	Creatinine	GFR	

Notes

GENERAL MEDICAL CENTER
CT Screening Form

Patient Name: *Margaret Walker*   **Referring Physician:** *Dr. Bettina Hawkins*

Sex: ☐ Male ☑ Female   **Height:** *5'6"*   **Weight:** *121 lbs*   **Age:** *52*

Are you pregnant? ☐ Yes ☑ No ☐ N/A   **Last menstrual period:** _____

Please explain the reason for which you are having a CT exam:
Neck pain
_____
_____

List other medical problems: *None*

List any drug and/or food allergies: *None*

Are you taking Gluaphage? ☐ Yes ☑ No   **BUN** _____   **Creatinine:** _____   **eGFR:** _____

Have you ever had a previous allergic reaction to x-ray contrast (dye)? ☐ Yes ☑ No

Have you been pre-medicated for this exam? ☐ Yes ☑ No

Do you have or have you ever had any of the following?

☐ Yes	☑ No	Asthma
☐ Yes	☑ No	Allergic Respiratory Disease
☐ Yes	☑ No	Diabetes
☐ Yes	☑ No	Kidney Disease
☐ Yes	☑ No	Cancer
☐ Yes	☑ No	Multiple Myeloma
☐ Yes	☑ No	Prostate Problems
☐ Yes	☑ No	Are you breast feeding at this time?
☐ Yes	☑ No	Dizziness
☐ Yes	☑ No	Heart Disease
☐ Yes	☑ No	Stroke
☐ Yes	☑ No	Liver Disease
☐ Yes	☑ No	Seizure Disorder
☐ Yes	☑ No	Bladder Disease
☑ Yes	☐ No	Headaches

List Previous Surgeries:
Hysterectomy
_____
_____
_____

List Medications Currently Taking:
Toradol
_____
_____
_____

I attest that the above information is correct to the best of my knowledge.

X *Margaret Walker*   _____   _____
Patient/Parent/Legal Guardian   **CT Technologist's Signature**   **Date**

FOR TECHNOLOGIST USE ONLY

Type of contrast: _____   **Contrast Temperature:** _____

Lot Number: _____   **Expiration Date:** _____

Time of Injection: _____   **Amount:** _____

Protocol

Protocol: CT Cervical Spine Post Myelogram

Parameters	Scout	Pre Contrast	Reconstructions
Patient Position	Supine	Supine	
Patient Entry	Head First	Head First	
Scan Type	Scout	Helical	
Scan Plane		Transverse	Sagittal
IV Contrast	N/A	N/A	
IV Contrast Timing	N/A	N/A	
IV Contrast Scan Delay	N/A	N/A	
Oral Contrast	N/A	N/A	
Reference Angle		No Gantry Tilt	
Scan Field of View		Large Body	
Display Field of View	50m	14cm	22cm
Start Location		Just above the skull base	
End Location		Mid T1	
Algorithm		Soft Tissue	Bone
Speed (mm/rot)		12.5	
Reconstruction Slice Thickness		2.5mm	2.0mm
Slice Spacing		1.25mm	2.0mm
Pitch		.625	
KV		140	
MA		125	
Detector Rows		16	

Slice Reference

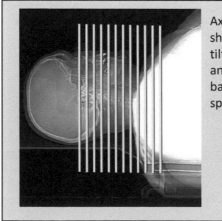

Axial slices of the cervical spine should be oriented with no gantry tilt. The slices should cover the anatomy from just above the skull base, through the entire cervical spine to the first thoracic vertebrae.

Patient Screening Questions:

1. Is the exam ordered consistent with the patient's history and symptoms? If not, describe why they are not consistent.

_____

_____

_____

_____

_____

_____

_____

2. Are there any contraindications that would prevent the patient from having a CT exam? If so, list and describe each.

_____

_____

_____

_____

_____

_____

_____

3. Are there any items found on the patient screening form that could cause potential artifacts? If so, please describe.

_____

_____

_____

_____

_____

_____

_____

Exam Performance Questions

4. Were there any artifacts on the images? If so, list the artifact name, list the sequence it appears on, describe its appearance, and define how it should be corrected.

_____

_____

_____

_____

_____

_____

5. Was there any pathology found on the images? If so, list the sequence it appears on and describe its appearance.

_____

_____

_____

_____

_____

6. What is the suggested time delay that should occur between the myelogram and the CT exam? Why is this delay necessary?

_____

_____

_____

_____

_____

7. Why should the patient be rolled on the table before the CT exam?

_____

_____

_____

_____

_____

NOTES

NOTES

CT Chest Without & With Contrast

Objective:

In this lab you will screen the patient, scan a CT of the chest without & with contrast, and evaluate the images.

Patient Information

Patient: Anthony Matthews
Age: 42
History: 42 y/o male with shortness of breath for 1 month.
Referring Physician: Katherine Ellis, MD

I. PATIENT SCREENING:

A. Evaluate the patient requisition.

B. Evaluate and sign the patient's screening form.

C. Answer the patient screening questions.

II. PERFORM EXAM:

A. If there are no contraindications, enter the patient's name and demographic information into the simulator and continue the exam performance steps. If there are contraindications, please halt the study.

C. Scan the protocol listed on page 4. Upon the completion of each sequence evaluate the images for artifacts and pathology.

D. Answer the procedure questions.

General Medical Center
Patient Requisition

Patient ID			Accession Number	
41256838			CT1505101748	

Last Name		First Name	Referring Physician	
Matthews		Anthony	Katherine Ellis, MD	

Age	Gender	Phone	Exam
42	M	(478)555-0808	CT Chest Without & With Contrast

History

42 y/o male with shortness of breath for 1 month.

BUN	Creatinine	GFR	
15.0	1.1	73.0	

Notes

GENERAL MEDICAL CENTER
CT Screening Form

Patient Name: _Anthony Matthews_   Referring Physician: _Dr. Katherine Ellis_

Sex: ☑Male ☐ Female   Height: _5'-10"_   Weight: _210 lbs_   Age: _42_

Are you pregnant? ☐Yes ☑No ☐N/A   Last menstrual period: _____

Please explain the reason for which you are having a CT exam:
Shortness of breath for 1 month

List other medical problems: _Prostate Cancer_

List any drug and/or food allergies: _None_

Are you taking Gluaphage? ☐Yes ☑No   BUN _15.0_   Creatinine: _1.1_   eGFR: _73.0_

Have you ever had a previous allergic reaction to x-ray contrast (dye)? ☐Yes ☑No

Have you been pre-medicated for this exam? ☐Yes ☑No

Do you have or have you ever had any of the following?

☑Yes ☐No	Asthma
☐Yes ☑No	Allergic Respiratory Disease
☐Yes ☑No	Diabetes
☐Yes ☑No	Kidney Disease
☑Yes ☐No	Cancer
☐Yes ☑No	Multiple Myeloma
☑Yes ☐No	Prostate Problems
☐Yes ☑No	Are you breast feeding at this time?
☐Yes ☑No	Dizziness
☐Yes ☑No	Heart Disease
☐Yes ☑No	Stroke
☐Yes ☑No	Liver Disease
☐Yes ☑No	Seizure Disorder
☐Yes ☑No	Bladder Disease
☐Yes ☑No	Headaches

List Previous Surgeries:
Prostate seed placement

List Medications Currently Taking:
None

I attest that the above information is correct to the best of my knowledge.

X _Anthony Matthews_ _____   _____   _____
   Patient/Parent/Legal Guardian   CT Technologist's Signature   Date

---

FOR TECHNOLOGIST USE ONLY

Type of contrast: _____   Contrast Temperature: _____

Lot Number: _____   Expiration Date: _____

Time of Injection: _____   Amount: _____

Protocol

Protocol: CT Chest Without & With Contrast

Parameters	Scout	Pre Contrast	Post Contrast	Reconstructions
Patient Position	Supine	Supine	Supine	
Patient Entry	Head First	Head First	Head First	
Scan Type		Helical	Helical	
Scan Plane		Transverse	Transverse	Axial
Beath Hold		Inspiration	Inspiration	
IV Contrast	N/A	N/A	80 mL @	
IV Contrast Timing	N/A	N/A	3.0 mL/s	
IV Contrast Scan Delay	N/A	N/A	35 Seconds	
Oral Contrast		N/A	N/A	
Reference Angle		No Gantry Tilt	No Gantry Tilt	
Scan Field of View		Large Body	Large Body	
Display Field of View	50cm	38cm	38cm	38 cm
Start Location		Just above lung apices	Just above lung apices	
End Location		Just below the costophrenic angles (if known or suspected Lung CA below the adrenal glands)	Just below the costophrenic angles (if known or suspected Lung CA below the adrenal glands)	
Algorithm		**Soft Tissue**	**Soft Tissue**	Bone
Speed (mm/rot)		27.0	27.0	
Reconstruction Slice Thickness		2.5 mm	2.5 mm	5mm
Slice Spacing		1.25 mm	1.25 mm	
Pitch		1.35	1.35	
KV		120	120	
MA		100-150	100-150	
Detector Rows		16	16	

Slice Reference

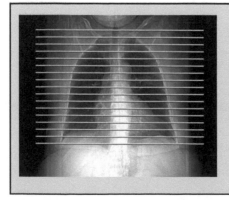

Transverse slices of the chest can be planned without gantry angulation and should cover the anatomy from just the lung apices to just below the costophrenic angles. If the patient has known or suspected lung cancer, slices should extend inferiorly through the adrenal glands.

Patient Screening Questions:

1. Is the exam ordered consistent with the patient's history and symptoms? If not, describe why they are not consistent.

_____

_____

_____

_____

_____

_____

_____

_____

2. Are there any contraindications that would prevent the patient from having a CT exam? If so, list and describe each.

_____

_____

_____

_____

_____

_____

_____

_____

3. Are there any items found on the patient screening form that could cause potential artifacts? If so, please describe.

_____

_____

_____

_____

_____

_____

_____

_____

Exam Performance Questions

4. Were there any artifacts on the images? If so, list the artifact name, list the sequence it appears on, describe its appearance, and define how it should be corrected.

_____

_____

_____

_____

_____

_____

5. Was there any pathology found on the images? If so, list the sequence it appears on and describe its appearance.

_____

_____

_____

_____

_____

6. Describe the High-resolution CT (HRCT) technique. What is the purpose of HRCT?

_____

_____

_____

_____

_____

7. What is the benefit of placing the patient in the prone position during a high-resolution CT of the chest.

_____

_____

_____

_____

_____

_____

_____

NOTES

NOTES

CT Chest With Contrast

Objective:

In this lab you will screen the patient, scan a CT of the chest with contrast, and evaluate the images.

Patient Information

Patient: Louis McGinnis
Age: 68
History: 68 y/o male with chest pain & shortness of breath x 4 days.
Referring Physician: Clifford Fry, MD

I. PATIENT SCREENING:

A. Evaluate the patient requisition.

B. Evaluate and sign the patient's screening form.

C. Answer the patient screening questions.

II. PERFORM EXAM:

A. If there are no contraindications, enter the patient's name and demographic information into the simulator and continue the exam performance steps. If there are contraindications, please halt the study.

B. Scan the protocol listed on page 4. Upon the completion of each sequence evaluate the images for artifacts and pathology.

D. Answer the procedure questions.

General Medical Center
Patient Requisition

Patient ID		Accession Number	
41256832		CT1505101739	

Last Name	First Name	Referring Physician
McGinnis	Louis	Clifford Fry, MD

Age	Gender	Phone	Exam
68	M	(478)555-0909	CT Chest With Contrast

History

68 y/o male with chest pain & shortness of breath x 4 days.
Rule out pulmonary embolism.

BUN	Creatinine	GFR	
14.0	1.2	60.0	

Notes

GENERAL MEDICAL CENTER
CT Screening Form

Patient Name: _Louis McGinnis_   **Referring Physician:** _Dr. Clifford Fry_

Sex: ☒ Male ☐ Female   **Height:** _60"_   **Weight:** _201 lbs_   **Age:** _68_

Are you pregnant? ☐ Yes ☒ No ☐ N/A   **Last menstrual period:** _____

Please explain the reason for which you are having a CT exam:
Chest pain & shortness of breath for 4 days

List other medical problems: _Arthritis_

List any drug and/or food allergies: _None_

Are you taking Gluaphage? ☐ Yes ☒ No   **BUN** _14.0_ **Creatinine:** _1.2_ **eGFR:** _60.0_

Have you ever had a previous allergic reaction to x-ray contrast (dye)? ☐ Yes ☒ No

Have you been pre-medicated for this exam? ☐ Yes ☒ No

Do you have or have you ever had any of the following?

☐ Yes	☒ No	Asthma
☐ Yes	☒ No	Allergic Respiratory Disease
☐ Yes	☒ No	Diabetes
☐ Yes	☒ No	Kidney Disease
☐ Yes	☒ No	Cancer
☐ Yes	☒ No	Multiple Myeloma
☐ Yes	☒ No	Prostate Problems
☐ Yes	☒ No	Are you breast feeding at this time?
☒ Yes	☐ No	Dizziness
☐ Yes	☒ No	Heart Disease
☐ Yes	☒ No	Stroke
☐ Yes	☒ No	Liver Disease
☐ Yes	☒ No	Seizure Disorder
☐ Yes	☒ No	Bladder Disease
☐ Yes	☒ No	Headaches

List Previous Surgeries:
Hip replacement 2 weeks ago

List Medications Currently Taking:
None

I attest that the above information is correct to the best of my knowledge.

X_____Louis McGinnis_____   _____   _____
Patient/Parent/Legal Guardian   **CT Technologist's Signature**   **Date**

FOR TECHNOLOGIST USE ONLY

Type of contrast: _____   **Contrast Temperature:** _____

Lot Number: _____   **Expiration Date:** _____

Time of Injection: _____   **Amount:** _____

Protocol

Protocol: CT Chest Without & With Contrast

Parameters	Scout	Post Contrast	Reconstructions
Patient Position	Supine	Supine	
Patient Entry	Head First	Head First	
Scan Type		Helical	Axial/Coronal/ Sagittal
Scan Plane		Transverse	
Beath Hold		Inspiration	
IV Contrast	N/A	80 mL @	
IV Contrast Timing	N/A	3.0 mL/s	
IV Contrast Scan Delay	N/A	35 Seconds	
Oral Contrast		N/A	
Reference Angle		No Gantry Tilt	
Scan Field of View		Large Body	
Display Field of View	50cm	38cm	38cm
Start Location		Just above lung apices	
End Location		Just below the costophrenic angles (if known or suspected Lung CA below the adrenal glands)	
Algorithm		Soft Tissue	Bone/Soft Tissue/ Soft Tissue
Speed mm/rot		27.0	
Reconstruction Slice Thickness		2.5 mm	1.5mm
Slice Spacing		1.25 mm	0 mm
Pitch		1.35	
KV		120	
MA		100-150	
Detector Rows		16	

Slice Reference

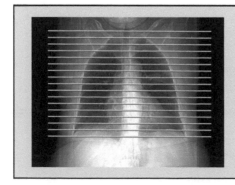

Transverse slices of the chest can be planned without gantry angulation and should cover the anatomy from just the lung apices to just below the costophrenic angles. If the patient has known or suspected lung cancer, slices should extend inferiorly through the adrenal glands.

Patient Screening Questions:

1. Is the exam ordered consistent with the patient's history and symptoms? If not, describe why they are not consistent.

_____

_____

_____

_____

_____

_____

_____

2. Are there any contraindications that would prevent the patient from having a CT exam? If so, list and describe each.

_____

_____

_____

_____

_____

_____

_____

_____

3. Are there any items found on the patient screening form that could cause potential artifacts? If so, please describe.

_____

_____

_____

_____

_____

_____

_____

_____

Exam Performance Questions

6. Were there any artifacts on the images? If so, list the artifact name, list the sequence it appears on, describe its appearance, and define how it should be corrected.

_____

_____

_____

_____

_____

_____

_____

_____

7. Was there any pathology found on the images? If so, list the sequence it appears on and describe its appearance.

_____

_____

_____

_____

_____

_____

_____

_____

8. Describe the appearance of a pulmonary embolism.

_____

_____

_____

_____

_____

_____

_____

_____

NOTES

NOTES

CT Chest With Contrast

Objective:

In this lab you will screen the patient, scan a CT of the chest with contrast, and evaluate the images.

Patient Information

Patient: Susan Blackwell
Age: 43
History: 43 y/o female with chest pains x 2 weeks, abnormal chest x-ray.
Referring Physician: Madison Nichols, MD

I. PATIENT SCREENING:

A. Evaluate the patient requisition.

B. Evaluate and sign the patient's screening form.

C. Answer the patient screening questions.

II. PERFORM EXAM:

A. If there are no contraindications, enter the patient's name and demographic information into the simulator and continue the exam performance steps. If there are contraindications, please halt the study.

B. Scan the protocol listed on page 4. Upon the completion of each sequence evaluate the images for artifacts and pathology.

C. Answer the procedure questions.

General Medical Center
Patient Requisition

Patient ID	Accession Number
41256832	CT1505101739

Last Name	First Name	Referring Physician
Blackwell	Susan	Madison Nichols, MD

Age	Gender	Phone	Exam
43	F	(478)555-1010	CT Chest With Contrast

History

43 y/o female with chest pains x 2 weeks, abnormal chest x-ray.

BUN	Creatinine	GFR	
18.0	1.1	54.0	

Notes

GENERAL MEDICAL CENTER
CT Screening Form

Patient Name: _Susan Blackwell_ **Referring Physician:** _Dr. Madison Nichols_

Sex: ☐ Male ☒ Female   **Height:** _5'2"_   **Weight:** _120 lbs_   **Age:** _43_

Are you pregnant? ☐ Yes ☒ No ☐ N/A   **Last menstrual period:** _____

Please explain the reason for which you are having a CT exam:
Chest pains for 2 weeks

List other medical problems: _None_

List any drug and/or food allergies: _None_

Are you taking Gluaphage? ☐ Yes ☒ No   **BUN** _18.0_   **Creatinine:** _1.1_   **eGFR:** _54.0_

Have you ever had a previous allergic reaction to x-ray contrast (dye)? ☐ Yes ☒ No

Have you been pre-medicated for this exam? ☐ Yes ☒ No

Do you have or have you ever had any of the following?

☐ Yes	☒ No	Asthma
☐ Yes	☒ No	Allergic Respiratory Disease
☐ Yes	☒ No	Diabetes
☐ Yes	☒ No	Kidney Disease
☐ Yes	☒ No	Cancer
☐ Yes	☒ No	Multiple Myeloma
☐ Yes	☒ No	Prostate Problems
☐ Yes	☒ No	Are you breast feeding at this time?
☐ Yes	☒ No	Dizziness
☐ Yes	☒ No	Heart Disease
☐ Yes	☒ No	Stroke
☐ Yes	☒ No	Liver Disease
☐ Yes	☒ No	Seizure Disorder
☐ Yes	☒ No	Bladder Disease
☐ Yes	☒ No	Headaches

List Previous Surgeries:
Shoulder surgery

List Medications Currently Taking:
None

I attest that the above information is correct to the best of my knowledge.

X _Susan Blackwell_

Patient/Parent/Legal Guardian   **CT Technologist's Signature**   **Date**

FOR TECHNOLOGIST USE ONLY

Type of contrast: _____   **Contrast Temperature:** _____

Lot Number: _____   **Expiration Date:** _____

Time of Injection: _____   **Amount:** _____

Protocol

Protocol: CT Chest With Contrast

Parameters	Scout	Post Contrast	Reconstructions
Patient Position	Supine	Supine	
Patient Entry	Head First	Head First	
Scan Type		Helical	
Scan Plane		Transverse	Axial/Coronal/ Sagittal
Beath Hold		Inspiration	
IV Contrast	N/A	80 mL @	
IV Contrast Timing	N/A	3.0 mL/s	
IV Contrast Scan Delay	N/A	35 Seconds	
Oral Contrast		N/A	
Reference Angle		No Gantry Tilt	
Scan Field of View	Large Body	Large Body	
Display Field of View	50cm	38cm	38 cm
Start Location		Just above lung apices	
End Location		Just below the costophrenic angles (if known or suspected Lung CA below the adrenal glands)	
Algorithm		Soft Tissue	Bone/ Soft Tissue/ Soft Tissue
Speed (mm/rot)		27.0	
Reconstruction Slice Thickness		2.5 mm	2.0mm/2.0mm /2.0mm
Slice Spacing		1.25 mm	
Pitch		1.35	
KV		120	
MA		100-150	
Detector Rows		16	

Slice Reference

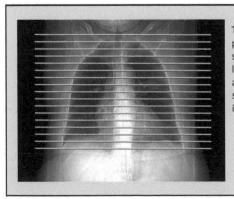

Transverse slices of the chest can be planned without gantry angulation and should cover the anatomy from just the lung apices to just below the costophrenic angles. If the patient has known or suspected lung cancer, slices should extend inferiorly through the adrenal glands.

Patient Screening Questions:

1. Is the exam ordered consistent with the patient's history and symptoms? If not, describe why they are not consistent.

_____

_____

_____

_____

_____

_____

_____

2. Are there any contraindications that would prevent the patient from having a CT exam? If so, list and describe each.

_____

_____

_____

_____

_____

_____

_____

_____

3. Are there any items found on the patient screening form that could cause potential artifacts? If so, please describe.

_____

_____

_____

_____

_____

_____

_____

Exam Performance Questions

4. Were there any artifacts on the images? If so, list the artifact name, list the sequence it appears on, describe its appearance, and define how it should be corrected.

_____

_____

_____

_____

_____

_____

_____

_____

5. Was there any pathology found on the images? If so, list the sequence it appears on and describe its appearance.

_____

_____

_____

_____

_____

_____

_____

_____

6. Why is it important to extend slices through the adrenal glands if patient has known or suspected lung cancer?

_____

_____

_____

_____

_____

_____

_____

_____

NOTES

NOTES

Objective:

In this lab you will screen the patient, scan a CT of the abdomen and pelvis without & with contrast, and evaluate the images.

Patient Information

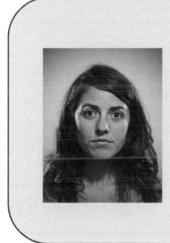

Patient: Ashley Williams
Age: 24
History: 24 y/o female with abdomen and pelvic pain for 6 days.
Referring Physician: Lauren Haley, MD

I. PATIENT SCREENING:

A. Evaluate the patient requisition.

B. Evaluate and sign the patient's screening form.

C. Answer the patient screening questions.

II. PERFORM EXAM:

A. If there are no contraindications, enter the patient's name and demographic information into the simulator and continue the exam performance steps. If there are contraindications, please halt the study.

B. Scan the protocol listed on page 4. Upon the completion of each sequence evaluate the images for artifacts and pathology.

C. Answer the procedure questions.

General Medical Center
Patient Requisition

Patient ID	Accession Number
41256841	CT1505101731

Last Name	First Name	Referring Physician
Williams	Ashley	Lauren Haley, MD

Age	Gender	Phone	Exam
24	F	(478)555-1010	CT Abdomen/Pelvis Without and With Cont

History

24 y/o female with abdomen and pelvic pain for 6 days.

BUN	Creatinine	GFR	
14.0	0.8	88.0	

Notes

GENERAL MEDICAL CENTER
CT Screening Form

Patient Name: _Ashley Williams_   Referring Physician: _Dr. Lauren Haley_

Sex: ☐Male ☑Female   Height: _59"_   Weight: _138 lbs_   Age: _24_

Are you pregnant? ☐Yes ☑No ☐N/A   Last menstrual period: _____

Please explain the reason for which you are having a CT exam:
Abdomen and pelvic pain for 6 days

List other medical problems: _None_

List any drug and/or food allergies: _Demerol_

Are you taking Gluaphage? ☐Yes ☑No   BUN _14.0_ Creatinine: _0.8_ eGFR: _88.0_

Have you ever had a previous allergic reaction to x-ray contrast (dye)? ☐Yes ☑No

Have you been pre-medicated for this exam? ☐Yes ☑No

Do you have or have you ever had any of the following?

☐Yes ☑No Asthma
☐Yes ☑No Allergic Respiratory Disease
☐Yes ☑No Diabetes
☐Yes ☑No Kidney Disease
☐Yes ☑No Cancer
☐Yes ☑No Multiple Myeloma
☐Yes ☑No Prostate Problems
☐Yes ☑No Are you breast feeding at this time?
☐Yes ☑No Dizziness
☐Yes ☑No Heart Disease
☐Yes ☑No Stroke
☐Yes ☑No Liver Disease
☐Yes ☑No Seizure Disorder
☐Yes ☑No Bladder Disease
☑Yes ☐No Headaches

List Previous Surgeries:
None

List Medications Currently Taking:
Lexapro, birth control

I attest that the above information is correct to the best of my knowledge.

X _Ashley Williams_ _____   _____   _____
  Patient/Parent/Legal Guardian   **CT Technologist's Signature**   **Date**

FOR TECHNOLOGIST USE ONLY

Type of contrast: _____   Contrast Temperature: _____

Lot Number: _____   Expiration Date: _____

Time of Injection: _____   Amount: _____

Protocol

Protocol: CT Abdomen/Pelvis Without & With Contrast

Parameters	Scout	Pre Contrast	Post Contrast	Reconstructions
Patient Position	Supine	Supine	Supine	
Patient Entry	Head First	Head First	Head First	
Scan Type		Helical	Helical	
Scan Plane		Transverse	Transverse	Coronal/ Sagittal
IV Contrast	N/A	N/A	125 mL @	
IV Contrast Timing	N/A	N/A	3.0 mL/s	
IV Contrast Scan Delay	N/A	N/A	65 Seconds	
Oral Contrast	N/A	675 ml Barium Sulfate	675 ml Barium Sulfate	
Reference Angle		No Gantry Angle	No Gantry Angle	
Scan Field of Vew		Large Body	Large Body	
Display Field of View	50 cm	38cm	38cm	38cm
Start Location		Just Above the Diaphragm	Just Above the Diaphragm	
End Location		Just Below the Symphysis Pubis	Just Below the Symphysis Pubis	
Algorithm		Soft Tissue	Soft Tissue	Soft Tissue
Speed (mm/rot)		27.0	27.0	
Reconstruction Slice Thickness		5mm	5mm	2mm
Slice Spacing		5mm	5mm	2mm
Pitch		1.35	1.35	
KV		120	120	
MA		≥230	≥230	
Detector Rows		16	16	

Slice Reference

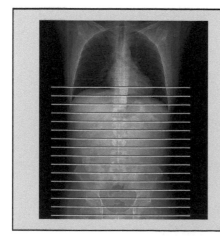

Transverse slices of the abdomen can be planned without gantry angulation. Slices should cover the anatomy from just above the diaphragm to just below the symphysis pubis.

Patient Screening Questions:

1. Is the exam ordered consistent with the patient's history and symptoms? If not, describe why they are not consistent.

_____

_____

_____

_____

_____

_____

_____

_____

2. Are there any contraindications that would prevent the patient from having a CT exam? If so, list and describe each.

_____

_____

_____

_____

_____

_____

_____

_____

3. Are there any items found on the patient screening form that could cause potential artifacts? If so, please describe.

_____

_____

_____

_____

_____

_____

_____

_____

Exam Performance Questions

4. Were there any artifacts on the images? If so, list the artifact name, list the sequence it appears on, describe its appearance, and define how it should be corrected.

_____

_____

_____

_____

_____

_____

_____

_____

_____

_____

_____

_____

5. Was there any pathology found on the images? If so, list the sequence it appears on and describe its appearance.

_____

_____

_____

_____

_____

_____

6. Why is it important to raise the patient's arms above their head during a CT exam of the abdomen?

_____

_____

_____

_____

_____

_____

_____

_____

NOTES

NOTES

CT Abdomen/Pelvis With Contrast

Objective:

In this lab you will screen the patient, scan a CT of the abdomen and pelvis with contrast, and evaluate the images.

Patient Information

Patient: Alfred Baker
Age: 66
History: 66 y/o male with diverticulosis, diarrhea, right sided abdomen and pelvis pain, fever and vomiting.
Referring Physician: Heather Mobley, MD

I. PATIENT SCREENING:

A. Evaluate the patient requisition.

B. Evaluate and sign the patient's screening form.

C. Answer the patient screening questions.

II. PERFORM EXAM:

A. If there are no contraindications, enter the patient's name and demographic information into the simulator and continue the exam performance steps. If there are contraindications, please halt the study.

B. Scan the protocol listed on page 4. Upon the completion of each sequence evaluate the images for artifacts and pathology.

C. Answer the procedure questions.

General Medical Center
Patient Requisition

Patient ID	Accession Number
95371	CT953713536

Last Name	First Name	Referring Physician
Baker	Alfred	Heather Mobley, MD

Age	Gender	Phone	Exam
66	M	(478)555-1212	CT Abdomen/Pelvis With Contrast

History

66 y/o male with diverticulosis, diarrhea, right sided abdomen and pelvis pain, fever and vomiting

BUN	Creatinine	GFR	
18.0	1.0	75.0	

Notes

GENERAL MEDICAL CENTER
CT Screening Form

Patient Name: _Alfred Baker_   **Referring Physician:** _Dr. Heather Mobley_

Sex: ☒ Male ☐ Female   **Height:** _57"_   **Weight:** _185 lbs_   **Age:** _66_

Are you pregnant? ☐ Yes ☐ No ☒ N/A   **Last menstrual period:** _____

Please explain the reason for which you are having a CT exam:
Diverticulosis, diarrhea, right-sided abdomen and pelvis pain, fever and vomiting

List other medical problems: _Cardiac pace maker, high cholesterol_

List any drug and/or food allergies: _Sulfa drugs_

Are you taking Gluaphage? ☐ Yes ☒ No   **BUN** _18.0_   **Creatinine:** _1.0_   **eGFR:** _75.0_

Have you ever had a previous allergic reaction to x-ray contrast (dye)? ☐ Yes ☒ No

Have you been pre-medicated for this exam? ☐ Yes ☒ No

Do you have or have you ever had any of the following?

☒ Yes ☐ No	Asthma	
☒ Yes ☐ No	Allergic Respiratory Disease	
☐ Yes ☒ No	Diabetes	
☐ Yes ☒ No	Kidney Disease	
☐ Yes ☒ No	Cancer	
☐ Yes ☒ No	Multiple Myeloma	
☐ Yes ☒ No	Prostate Problems	
☐ Yes ☒ No	Are you breast feeding at this time?	
☐ Yes ☒ No	Dizziness	
☒ Yes ☐ No	Heart Disease	
☐ Yes ☒ No	Stroke	
☒ Yes ☐ No	Liver Disease	
☐ Yes ☒ No	Seizure Disorder	
☐ Yes ☒ No	Bladder Disease	
☐ Yes ☒ No	Headaches	

List Previous Surgeries:
Gallbladder surgery, Heart surgery

List Medications Currently Taking:
Cymbalta, WelChol, promethazine, alprazolam,

I attest that the above information is correct to the best of my knowledge.

X _Alfred Baker_ _____   _____   _____
Patient/Parent/Legal Guardian   **CT Technologist's Signature**   **Date**

FOR TECHNOLOGIST USE ONLY

Type of contrast: _____   **Contrast Temperature:** _____

Lot Number: _____   **Expiration Date:** _____

Time of Injection: _____   **Amount:** _____

Protocol

Protocol: CT Abdomen/Pelvis With Contrast

Parameters	Scout	Post Contrast	Delayed Images	Reconstructions
Patient Position	Supine	Supine	Supine	
Patient Entry	Head First	Head First	Head First	
Scan Type		Helical	Helical	
Scan Plane		Transverse	Transverse	Coronal/Sagittal
IV Contrast	N/A	125 mL @		
IV Contrast Timing	N/A	3.0 mL/s		
IV Contrast Scan Delay	N/A	65 Seconds		
Oral Contrast	N/A	675 ml Barium Sulfate		
Reference Angle		No Gantry Angle	No Gantry Angle	
Scan Field of View		Large Body	Large Body	
Display Field of View	50 cm	38cm	38cm	38cm
Start Location		Just above the diaphragm	Just above the diaphragm	
End Location		Just below the symphysis pubis	Just below the iliac crest	
Algorithm		Soft Tissue	Soft Tissue	Soft Tissue
Speed (mm/rot)		27.0	27..0	
Reconstruction Slice Thickness		5mm	5mm	2mm
Slice Spacing		5mm	5mm	2mm
Pitch		1.35	1.35	
KV		120	120	
MA		≥230	≥230	
Detector Rows		16	16	

Slice Reference

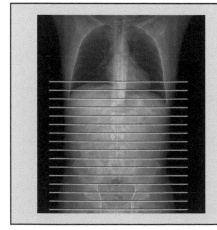

Transverse slices of the abdomen can be planned without gantry angulation. Slices should cover the anatomy from just above the diaphragm to just below the symphysis pubis.

Patient Screening Questions:

1. Is the exam ordered consistent with the patient's history and symptoms? If not, describe why they are not consistent.

_____

_____

_____

_____

_____

_____

_____

_____

2. Are there any contraindications that would prevent the patient from having a CT exam? If so, list and describe each.

_____

_____

_____

_____

_____

_____

_____

_____

3. Are there any items found on the patient screening form that could cause potential artifacts? If so, please describe.

_____

_____

_____

_____

_____

_____

_____

_____

Exam Performance Questions

4. Were there any artifacts on the images? If so, list the artifact name, list the sequence it appears on, describe its appearance, and define how it should be corrected.

_____

_____

_____

_____

_____

_____

_____

_____

5. Was there any pathology found on the images? If so, list the sequence it appears on and describe its appearance.

_____

_____

_____

_____

_____

_____

_____

_____

6. Identify and describe the 3 phases of contrast enhancement in the Liver?

_____

_____

_____

_____

_____

_____

_____

_____

NOTES

NOTES

Objective:
In this lab you will screen the patient, scan a CT of the lumbar spine without contrast, and evaluate the images.

Patient Information
Patient: Sophia Robinson
Age: 64
History: 64 y/o female with lower back pain.
Referring Physician: Ashley Hargett , MD

I. PATIENT SCREENING:

A. Evaluate the patient requisition.

B. Evaluate and sign the patient's screening form.

C. Answer the patient screening questions.

II. PERFORM EXAM:

A. If there are no contraindications, enter the patient's name and demographic information into the simulator and continue the exam performance steps. If there are contraindications, please halt the study.

B. Scan the protocol listed on page 4. Upon the completion of each sequence evaluate the images for artifacts and pathology.

C. Answer the procedure questions.

General Medical Center
Patient Requisition

Patient ID		Accession Number
356003		CT35600343589

Last Name	First Name	Referring Physician
Robinson	Sophia	Ashley Hargett , MD

Age	Gender	Phone	Exam
64	F	(478)555-1313	CT Lumbar Spine Without Contrast

History

64 y/o female with lower back pain.

BUN	Creatinine	GFR	

Notes

GENERAL MEDICAL CENTER
CT Screening Form

Patient Name: _Sophia Robinson_   **Referring Physician:** _Dr. Ashley Hargett_

Sex: ☐ Male ☑ Female   **Height:** _51"_   **Weight:** _105 lbs_   **Age:** _64_

Are you pregnant? ☐ Yes ☑ No ☐ N/A   **Last menstrual period:** _____

Please explain the reason for which you are having a CT exam:
Lower back pain

List other medical problems: _Arthritis, breast cancer_

List any drug and/or food allergies: _None_

Are you taking Gluaphage? ☐ Yes ☑ No   **BUN** _____   **Creatinine:** _____   **eGFR:** _____

Have you ever had a previous allergic reaction to x-ray contrast (dye)? ☐ Yes ☑ No

Have you been pre-medicated for this exam? ☐ Yes ☑ No

Do you have or have you ever had any of the following?

☐ Yes	☑ No	Asthma
☐ Yes	☑ No	Allergic Respiratory Disease
☐ Yes	☑ No	Diabetes
☐ Yes	☑ No	Kidney Disease
☑ Yes	☐ No	Cancer
☐ Yes	☑ No	Multiple Myeloma
☐ Yes	☑ No	Prostate Problems
☐ Yes	☑ No	Are you breast feeding at this time?
☐ Yes	☑ No	Dizziness
☐ Yes	☑ No	Heart Disease
☐ Yes	☑ No	Stroke
☐ Yes	☑ No	Liver Disease
☐ Yes	☑ No	Seizure Disorder
☐ Yes	☑ No	Bladder Disease
☐ Yes	☑ No	Headaches

List Previous Surgeries:
Mastectomy

List Medications Currently Taking:
Prilosec, aspirin, Lortab, Flexeril

I attest that the above information is correct to the best of my knowledge.

X _Sophia Robinson_

Patient/Parent/Legal Guardian   **CT Technologist's Signature**   **Date**

FOR TECHNOLOGIST USE ONLY

Type of contrast: _____   **Contrast Temperature:** _____

Lot Number: _____   **Expiration Date:** _____

Time of Injection: _____   **Amount:** _____

Protocol

Protocol: CT Lumbar Spine Without Contrast

Parameters	Scout	Pre Contrast	Reconstructions
Patient Position	Supine	Supine	
Patient Entry	Head First	Head First	
Scan Type		Helical	
Scan Plane		Transverse	Axial, Coronal, Sagittal
IV Contrast	N/A	N/A	
IV Contrast Timing	N/A	N/A	
IV Contrast Scan Delay	N/A	N/A	
Oral Contrast	N/A	N/A	
Reference Angle		No Gantry Tilt	
Scan Field of View		Large Body	
Display Field of View	50cm	16cm	16cm/28cm/28cm
Start Location		Just above L1	
End Location		Just Below S1	
Algorithm		Soft Tissue	Bone
Speed (mm/rot)		12.5	
Reconstruction Slice Thickness		2.5mm	3mm /1mm/1mm
Slice Spacing		1.25mm	3mm/1mm/1mm
Pitch		.625	
KV		140	
MA		150	
Detector Rows		16	

Slice Reference

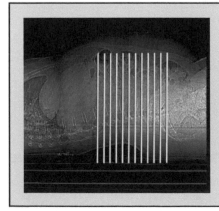

Transverse slices of the lumbar can be planned with no gantry angulation. The slices should cover the anatomy from just above L1 to just below S1.

Patient Screening Questions:

1. Is the exam ordered consistent with the patient's history and symptoms? If not, describe why they are not consistent.

_____

_____

_____

_____

_____

_____

_____

2. Are there any contraindications that would prevent the patient from having a CT exam? If so, list and describe each.

_____

_____

_____

_____

_____

_____

_____

3. Are there any items found on the patient screening form that could cause potential artifacts? If so, please describe.

_____

_____

_____

_____

_____

_____

_____

_____

Exam Performance Questions

4. Were there any artifacts on the images? If so, list the artifact name, list the sequence it appears on, describe its appearance, and define how it should be corrected.

_____

_____

_____

_____

_____

_____

_____

_____

6. Was there any pathology found on the images? If so, list the sequence it appears on and describe its appearance.

_____

_____

_____

_____

_____

_____

_____

_____

6. Describe when CT is superior to MRI exams in the spine?

_____

_____

_____

_____

_____

_____

_____

_____

NOTES

NOTES

Objective:

In this lab you will screen the patient, scan a CT of the wrist, and evaluate the images.

Patient Information

Patient: Emma Stewart
Age: 34
History: 34 y/o female with right wrist pain after injury 2 days ago.
Referring Physician: LeAnn Michaels, MD

I. PATIENT SCREENING:

A. Evaluate the patient requisition.

B. Evaluate and sign the patient's screening form.

C. Answer the patient screening questions.

II. PERFORM EXAM:

A. If there are no contraindications, enter the patient's name and information into the simulator and continue the exam performance steps. If there are contraindications, please halt the study.

B. Scan the protocol listed on page 4. Upon the completion of each sequence evaluate the images for artifacts and pathology.

C. Answer the procedure questions.

General Medical Center
Patient Requisition

Patient ID		Accession Number
88576		CT88576150

Last Name	First Name	Referring Physician
Stewart	Emma	LeAnn Michaels, MD

Age	Gender	Phone	Exam
34	F	(478)555-1414	CT Left Wrist

History

34 y/o female with left wrist pain after injury 2 days ago.

BUN	Creatinine	GFR	
0.00	0.00	0.00	

Notes

GENERAL MEDICAL CENTER
CT Screening Form

Patient Name: _Emma Stewart_   **Referring Physician:** _Dr. LeAnn Michaels_

Sex: ☐ Male ☑ Female   **Height:** _5'7"_   **Weight:** _138 lbs_   **Age:** _34_

Are you pregnant? ☐ Yes ☑ No ☐ N/A   **Last menstrual period:** _____

Please explain the reason for which you are having a CT exam:
Right wrist pain after injury 2 days ago

List other medical problems: _None_
List any drug and/or food allergies: _Shell fish_

Are you taking Gluaphage? ☐ Yes ☑ No   **BUN** _____ **Creatinine:** _____ **eGFR:** _____

Have you ever had a previous allergic reaction to x-ray contrast (dye)? ☐ Yes ☑ No

Have you been pre-medicated for this exam? ☐ Yes ☑ No

Do you have or have you ever had any of the following?

			List Previous Surgeries:
☐ Yes	☑ No	Asthma	_None_
☐ Yes	☑ No	Allergic Respiratory Disease	
☐ Yes	☑ No	Diabetes	
☐ Yes	☑ No	Kidney Disease	
☐ Yes	☑ No	Cancer	
☐ Yes	☑ No	Multiple Myeloma	
☐ Yes	☑ No	Prostate Problems	**List Medications Currently Taking:**
☐ Yes	☑ No	Are you breast feeding at this time?	_None_
☐ Yes	☑ No	Dizziness	
☐ Yes	☑ No	Heart Disease	
☐ Yes	☑ No	Stroke	
☐ Yes	☑ No	Liver Disease	
☐ Yes	☑ No	Seizure Disorder	
☐ Yes	☑ No	Bladder Disease	
☐ Yes	☑ No	Headaches	

I attest that the above information is correct to the best of my knowledge.

X _Emma Stewart_ _____   _____   _____
   Patient/Parent/Legal Guardian   **CT Technologist's Signature**   **Date**

FOR TECHNOLOGIST USE ONLY

Type of contrast: _____   **Contrast Temperature:** _____

Lot Number: _____   **Expiration Date:** _____

Time of Injection: _____   **Amount:** _____

Protocol

Protocol: CT Wrist

Parameters	Scout	Pre Contrast	Reconstructions
Patient Position	Prone	Prone	
Patient Entry	Head First	Head First	
Scan Type	Scout	Helical	
Scan Plane	AP/Lateral	Transverse	Coronal
IV Contrast	N/A	N/A	
IV Contrast Timing	N/A	N/A	
IV Contrast Scan Delay	N/A	N/A	
Oral Contrast	N/A	N/A	
Reference Angle		No Gantry Angle	
Scan Field of View	Large Body	Large Body	
Display Field of View	50cm	10cm	10cm
Start Location		Just proximal to distal radioulnar joint	
End Location		At proximal metacarpals	
Algorithm		Bone	Bone
Speed (mm/rot)		12.5	
Reconstruction Slice Thickness		0.625mm	2mm
Slice Spacing		0.3mm	0mm
Pitch		.625	
KV		140	
MA		300	
Detector Rows		16	

Slice Reference

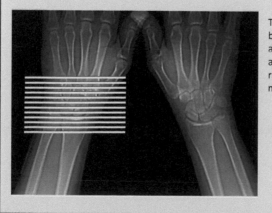

Transverse slices of the wrist can be planned with no gantry angulation. Slices should cover the anatomy from Just proximal to the radioulnar joint to the proximal metacarpals.

Patient Screening Questions:

1. Is the exam ordered consistent with the patient's history and symptoms? If not, describe why they are not consistent.

_____

_____

_____

_____

_____

_____

_____

2. Are there any contraindications that would prevent the patient from having a CT exam? If so, list and describe each.

_____

_____

_____

_____

_____

_____

_____

3. Are there any items found on the patient screening form that could cause potential artifacts? If so, please describe.

_____

_____

_____

_____

_____

_____

_____

Exam Performance Questions

4. Were there any artifacts on the images? If so, list the artifact name, list the sequence it appears on, describe its appearance, and define how it should be corrected.

_____

_____

_____

_____

_____

_____

_____

_____

5. Was there any pathology found on the images? If so, list the sequence it appears on and describe its appearance.

_____

_____

_____

_____

_____

_____

_____

_____

6. Describe why it is extremely important to properly label CT exams of the wrist?

_____

_____

_____

_____

_____

_____

_____

NOTES

NOTES